THE WATER TABLE

Philip Gross was born in 1952 in Delabole, Cornwall. Professor of Creative Writing at Glamorgan University, he has taught writing at every step on the educational ladder from nursery to PhD, and relishes collaboration with musicians, dancers and visual artists of all kinds. A Quaker who has also written horror and science fiction, children's opera and radio plays, he now lives with his wife Zélie in Penarth

Since winning a Gregory Award in 1981 and first prize in the National Poetry Competition in 1982 he has published books with Peterloo, Faber and Bloodaxe, including *The Air Mines of Mistila*, with Sylvia Kantaris (1988: Poetry Book Society Choice) and *The Wasting Game* (1998: shortlisted for the Whitbread Poetry Award). Poems from all these and several small-press collections are brought together in *Changes of Address: Poems 1980-1998* (Bloodaxe Books, 2001). His latest collections are *Mappa Mundi* (2003), a Poetry Book Society Recom-mendation, *The Egg of Zero* (2006), and *The Water Table* (2009) – all from Bloodaxe – and *I Spy Pinhole Eye*, a collaboration with photographer Simon Denison, from Cinnamon (2009).

His poetry for children includes *Manifold Manor, The All-Nite Café* (winner of the Signal Award 1994) and *Scratch City*, all from Faber, who also published his first novel for young people, *The Song of Gail and Fludd*, in 1991. Since then he has published nine more, with Scholastic and with Oxford University Press – most recently *The Storm Garden* (2006).

PHILIP GROSS

THE WATER TABLE

BLOODAXE BOOKS

ISBN: 978 1 85224 852 9

First published 2009 by
Bloodaxe Books Ltd,
Highgreen,
Tarset,
Northumberland NE48 1RP.

www.bloodaxebooks.com
For further information about Bloodaxe titles
please visit our website or write to
the above address for a catalogue.

Supported by
ARTS COUNCIL
ENGLAND

Cover design: Neil Astley & Pamela Robertson-Pearce.

Printed in Great Britain by
Bell & Bain Limited, Glasgow, Scotland.

For Zélie, and for all our families:

– the sky is in the house
and all the doors are blowing open –

ACKNOWLEDGEMENTS

Acknowledgements are due to the editors of the following publications in which some of these poems first appeared: *Blackbird, The Bow-Wow Shop, Contourlines* (Salt Publishing, 2009), *Feeling the Pressure: poetry and science of climate change*, ed. Paul Munden (British Council, 2008), *Friends Quarterly, London Magazine, Magma, Moment of Earth: poems and essays in honour of Jeremy Hooker*, ed. Christopher Meredith (Celtic Studies Publications, 2007), *New Welsh Review, Pendulum: The Poetry of Dreams*, ed. Deborah Gaye (Avalanche Books, 2008), *Planet, Poetry Daily, Poetry Review, Poetry Wales, The Rialto, Scintilla, Smartish Pace, Smith's Knoll, Stand, Swansea Review* and *Warwick Review*.

CONTENTS

Sluice Angel

Low tide at the sea lock,
      a forty foot drop to muddy shallows...
          One boat's width

      of channel that the dredger grubs up
          daily... Silt to one side scored in circles

          where they dragged for don't ask what...

The tall shut doors of the hall
      of the world at which the wuight of watci,
          of *incipience*, does not need to knock:

      feel it there like a shudder
          of difference, the engine of change.

          Now, almost soundless, hinges shift.

With a gradual calibrated rip
      like a concord of lathes, with a crypt smell,
          two green-grey-brown stiffening blades

      of water fold in. They curve, feathering
          themselves in free fall: wings

          flexed, shuddering, not to soar

but to pour themselves down, to earth
      the charge, liquid solid as rock
          and untouchable, trouncing itself

      to a froth, to exhaustion, till with a sigh
          the gates can open, and the world,

          our world, small craft, come through.

Betweenland I

A body of water: water's body

that seems to have a mind (and
change it: isn't that what makes

a *mind*, its changing?) not much
prone to thinking – rather, thoughts
curl through it, salt or fresh, or hang

between states; sometimes gloss
the surface with their oil-illuminations.

Wind-worried to dullness, pulled two ways
(earth and moon like parents not quite
in accord), unquiet body, it can never

quite lay down its silt; always trying
to be something other, to be sky,

to lose itself in absolute reflection.

Betweenland II

Mud,
     the megatonnage of it, moving
in suspension, heavy haulage, to and fro.
A weight you can see,
               the way it stands
off the Point, its deep whorls scarcely
moving, scarcelyly filling:
           clay shapes
turned on a wheel, leather hard already. One
spins off now like a slow world,
                 like a question
about nothing it can put a name to,
                   an expression
that leaves home in search of a face of its own.

White Sheet

Note to self: might have to work
to break the beauty of white pages:
not much gets conceived
on an unsullied sheet.

Might have to sweat it a bit – not,
not in bounden duty but
with all the ruthless lack
of circumspection

of pure play

        *

        (that night for instance

in my parents' plasterboard box-room
when we let a whey-faced moon

loom in on us all night,
its low arc the width of the window,

nudging the cloud-flow, shift-
and-shuffling its shadows of us

on the wall behind the bed,
those above-and-beyonders, other-lovers,

the immortals on the white sheet
of the shadow-puppet screen – and us

the crouched mechanicals beneath
who give themselves up, hands, eyes and skill,

as their parents did and theirs and theirs,
to make them... dare I say *real*?)

        *

Some mornings I
        find spider-writing
on my bedside pad

        as lucid
as a doctor's script.

No, dreams are not the mystery.

The thing is waking.
        Note to self

from other: Here, today
        let us misunderstand
each other

                giftedly.

Atlantis World

One day the sea thought *No*. It wouldn't. Just wouldn't. It withdrew
to the doors of the straits, like an Ice Age instituted overnight,
like an empire in-turned behind walls of glittering indifference
    to the mess outside.

And where did that leave *us*? Facing into the space between
redundant coastlines – space, a vast parcel we'd come down to find
at the ring of a doorbell, nobody's birthday, and giftwrapped
    in silksilver mud.

The seabed smell had started rising, that of secrets being out;
like any seedy leakage in the press there would be more to come.
It wasn't the way we had dreamed it: alluvial pastures unfolded
    from our inward valleys,

restored from our national childhoods. Those who'd hoped for free
smallholdings for the homeless, and those already drafting the adverts
for Atlantis World, we'd all be disappointed. As the sun came up
    it was already baking,

the mud going matt, then wrinkling, firing itself like epic pottery.
Tiny islands came into their own, as grass-topped mountains,
the one with the lighthouse a marvel: Monte Lucia, heraldic.
    Trickles cut down deep

in muddy gulches, going on for canyons. Round the middle slopes,
the beaches were considering a new career as archaeology,
waterfront apartments rebranding themselves as mountain
    villages like Tuscany.

The piers seemed naked, their black-weedy legs embarrassing,
due for a shave. Work redoubled on long-planned sea walls
in case rains washed us down in mudslides like some peasant
    valley worlds away;

we didn't want to go there. Somebody was bussing in scanty-paid
somebodies-else already, to pick across the wastes with hammers,
chipping out crabs, skirting the bones of burials at sea, a horse,
    a child from steerage;

then that crop was gone. A few sunk ships were there to be avoided
like war graves and, as if that had jogged some recollection, each
side sent in surveyors, just to clarify the border. Seeing which,
    a discreet small column

followed, lightly armoured, as the wind got up and mud dust
started swirling round them, like in any desert, and first shots
were fired, as a precaution mainly. The sea gave an audible sigh
    and came back in.

Designs for the Water Garden

1

            : glass stepping stones,
flat topped, level with the water,
so on mornings after, when a low
mist frosts the lake, the host walks
out towards the island where black
coffee waits; he calls the guests, o
ye of little faith, to join him.

2

            : a rain-gazebo
with a narrow ceiling-well and a grille
in the floor, so whatever the sky sends
stands in our midst, passing through,
a slim visitor, greyish and graceful
and slightly distrait. We receive her
politely, but she never stops for tea.

3

            : a salmon treadwheel
where the fish in season thrashes up
the water-stair, bucket by bucket, each
time tripping the house-high millwheel
down a click. A noble fate. Like us,
it thrives on purpose, always getting
somewhere, never (*what now?*) done.

4

            : a mist maze –
with aerosol-fine fountains to infuse
the walled garden with varying densities
from slight pearling to period pea-souper.
In winter, bare trees seem to pace the maze
amongst us. For the children there's always
a rainbow or two. We keep them like pets.

5

      : the eel scene.
Just *be* there, drive through wind and rain,
whichever night's the night. The eels are struggling
in their caged sluice. Now! We pop the bubbly,
frothing. They pour west, released into their instincts,
a slow gusher, oilily across the lawn, around
our shucked clothes in the mud, our naked feet.

6

      : a flood-feature
like a force-field carved in silt and stuff:
the tracks of the water-beast dragging its bulk
through the garden. Its scrapings, its droppings,
twig-mats and shreddings wrapped round trees.
We contemplate it, for our own good. This is Art
and this is England and the river's miles away.

7

      : a water-glass lens
though which you can see only water.
All the rest, dark matter... Here's the stream
through which light enters the world; there,
its tree-shaped escape to the sky; here, walking
through the night of dryness, we're revealed
as lattices of mostly water, flowing side by side.

Almost Alabaster
(for Zélie, in Penarth)

Mudstone, grey-green and oxblood,
        dun crusts of limestone interleaved

and a wavering white-dotted-tide-
        line, somewhere between centuries:

gypsum, crisp as a fossilised foam.
        Beneath this long pitch, yaw and swell

of strata, steady me; it's the slow
        upheaving, it's the way the most amenable

houses in town seem to ride up the Head
        just to crumble: a gazebo, railings, terraces

of hanging gardens contemplate the edge.
        A slight wind, and fine grit disperses

warnings. White, buff, pink chunks on the beach:
        each morning leaves gifts in the casual way

a cat presents small slaughter at your feet
        expecting thanks. Mute lumps: the waves'

sucked sweeties, coarse peppermint, coconut
        ice – crude figurines, tongue-sculptures

licked half into shape like words not
        quite articulate. So close, so almost *alabaster*,

they're not quite or only in passing the virginal
        white collectors prize. Blotched and liver-

spotted, with the ambiguous shadow-and-blush
        of a cinema curtain's flounces, with mud, rust

and verdigris, the bleeding-in of beautiful
        impurities, these are for us.

Fantasia on a Theme from IKEA
seven descants on 'ground'

(for Jeremy Hooker)

We could see ourselves in one, these half-a-rooms
of dolls'-house lifestyle, life-sized (the books on the shelves
in Swedish). We order by numbers; down in catacombs
a forklift whirrs down the racks of available selves.
We follow the way-marked route at a shuffling shunt
round each turn, like the Ghost Train in a seaside fair –
for miles, then stumble out into... astonishment
to see, after all, it's just a shed. Take a square
box, corrugated over girders; blue and yellow paint;
a brown-field site, a name... And it has become
a world, born of economies of scale, ground rent,
need and desire: the product of the sum
of (as real and recurrent as mist from the stream
the car park buried) *us* – the human dream.

*

Dream on! The girl in the car park snaps
her phone shut. End of story. She folds him away,
the face on a screen like a make-up mirror; slaps
him in her hipster pocket, snug – which may
be as close as he'll get (and yet not know)
to what he's dreamed of. Her, she's had enough.
Behind her, billboards plead: Dream *this*. So
much they need us, dreams. We are such stuff:
flesh, matter. No wonder they can't look away,
all those ideals and angels. Where else to found
their celestial cities but on grit and clay,
hormones and DNA? Where else to ground
their being? The phone in her pocket chirrs, cheep
cheep. Poor lovebird. She puts it to sleep.

*

Sleep is something like it: what ground does
beneath our soles. It breathes. Sometimes it seems
to shift or shrug. It's not thinking, and not about us.
We are its slight disturbance – like most dreams
the product of qualms, hungers, physical itches
and aches, sometimes bearing gifts, vignettes
from the flipside of sense; more often, repetitious
buttonholings, boredom. Ground, like sleep, forgets
for a living. It's not that *the worm forgives
the plough*; it gives it *no mind*. (Pain
occurs, in passing.) Faced with a creature that lives
in, digests, shits, *creates* earth…how to explain
your self, this figure that steps from the ground and confronts
you in your own shape, saying: *This, this once?*

*

Once there was a figure who lived in a ground
(the plot was small but it was grand)
with a ditch and a bank and a burial mound.
I'll sing you a lay of the lie of the land,
derry down. He watched the red sun sink.
His shadow grew tall and skewed and thin.
It moved; he stayed; it made him think
and now the past was about to begin
as he looked for himself: where had he gone
while he stood there still as a standing stone
or a figure in chalk, oh, once upon
a down, derry down? But how he'd grown.
Thus time. Space. Relativity.
And so we are lonely, and elsewhere, and free.

*

Freehand, by eye, the master of his art
describes a circle. Without words. And again,
left handed. Bows to the assembled court
in silence. Outside, medieval rain
slows to a tick. Torch-flicker. *Fetch
the instruments!* A glance, cleric to lord,
lord to sergeant at arms. And now they watch

as the charcoal marks are measured, and declared
to be true. Too true. The verdict: theft
from God's perfection – no gift this, but craft,
a dark art. Guilty. Seized and bound.
Outside, a raindrop in the ditch articulates
no end of circles. Tethered to its stake
a cow crops circles from the thistly ground.

*

Groundlings, in the pit. Above, tier on tier,
to the gods, to a circle of sky. It's our sweat
and guffaws, our pulse, that oils the gears
that turn the Globe. The wheel of fire. (Yet
soft, what light?) The music of the spheres
sounds frail without a ground bass. It needs us
like we need a good grand downfall. Cheers.
Our revels now. We sway out, word-drunk, a tinnitus
hiss in our ears, the palpable hush of our blood
or, suddenly, the river. Sounds, crisp, far
apart. Mist does that. Breathes from the mud.
Brings things back. Where the lost streams are.
The ground's half water, like us. Piss at the wall,
slops from a window. It accepts us, one and all.

*

All Souls, tonight... Will that be us, those finished
articles, stacked round the shop floor of this life
gazing in: *souls?* Tempting to hope, as we're diminished
bit by (age, chance, illness, surgeon's knife)
bit. We will not be mended. Is that *growing*
up, at last, at least – to know we've begun
to disperse (did, from the start), our moments flowing
out, into and through each other, property of no one
any more than words or water... and into the ground-
swell of the sea like hills, or hills like sea,
in which we'd hoped to stand out like that down-
land figure, though he's just a chalk line round
an absence? We're elsewhere, we're home, if we
could step back far enough, if we could see.

Betweenland III

After rain,
            the far
shore – close,
with an almost accusing
acuity,
    as if nothing
could ever be ignored
again:
    every detail
(the tick of a wind-
turbine's vane
against the skyline)
a point it insists on:
                    no
no *no*, let me explain.

Coming To

A hundred-year-old steamer
puts in at the end of the pier –
        spick-liveried, navy and white,
        and sporting a thin gold trim,
a hint of epaulettes. High tide,

and it's almost the longest day
just ending, more light
        in the sea than the sky,
        more recollection than reflection.
A century late,

they seem expected: some
few on the deck, not quite
        together, not crew, not
        quite cargo, not a queue,
gaze at some other few who wait.

It might be an exchange of hostages.
(If there's a war, of a diffuse
        undeclared and understated nature,
        between Now and Then, this
evening and this light says *Truce*.)

                    Beside and apart, one crewman
                        totes a furred thick noose
                            as he judges the –
                                now –
                        lassoes
                    a bollard and (just by leaning:
                        he's not young himself)
                            hand-hauls it in.
                                That dream-
                            like weight-
                        lessness of steel consents. Is
            led. Bumps, and comes to.

And here I am, and now...and then
and then again: twelve metres
          and six hours below

at the mud's edge by the dry-shod
and barnacle-booted last legs of the pier,
          the dizzying idea

of depth above me where the anyway-
unlikely craft has moored
          suspended in mid-air

like an airship or our disbelief.
Up on the gangplank, one day-trip-dazed
          returner hesitates

(Look down, he'll feel my gaze
parting the grainy miasma of silt)
          before trusting his weight

to things, deciding to believe
in time and destinations.
          (Else, where would we be?)

Stilt City

Come down – lulled
by the puck-puck of piledrivers
(short-breathed, heart missing a beat)

where the nearly-new precinct
has been thrown in like a poor deal
and reshuffled. Let

thought thicken. (Slowed
to trees' pace we'd hear human speech
like birdsong, birdsong

as an insect whine.)
Now, mind
like water, sink

through earth-mist, silt-marsh, reed-mulch and salt pastures
where three rivers used to graze.
Now, promenade

among the straight-up forty-metre-
from-the-bedrock underpinnings, trunks
like a conifer glade, or the stilts

of a lagoon-side fishing village
and the twenty-storey
towers up there

are an early mythology, dreaming
itself upwards, robed
in glass, which you

in slow-time can perceive as liquid,
as fountains, a glittering
substance thrown into the light and

falling
          at its own pace
                                as a sheen
or now and then
in a shiver and puff, a bubble
burst, a dissipating spray.

Ware

        Between the making
of it and the breaking,
                        interleaved,

we are what you won't find,
you fastidious digger:
                        what was

spilled, contained and spilled again,
each spill a generation.
                        Ware

is what you're left with, roughly
fired and incised,
                        this hint of a *lip*

or a *lug*
            as if the language thought

this clay could speak or hear.

Betweenland IV

A *mouth*, we say – as if it spoke the hills'
native language in the lowlands' slow
translation. It's all hearsay:
a mountain hands down utterance
on all sides: no water belongs.

Only catchment, maybe, is a sort
of *self*, a notional line
within which nothing is alien to a river:
runoffs and bosky rivulets, storm drains
and spills, precipitation filtered though

our million bodies. And the mouth
debouches – all our secrets, for our old
twice daily, her who comes in and does,
to mop up. (Some of the juicier morsels
do the rounds like gossip, day by day.)

Boffins

Rabbit pasture. A low cove. A hint of a beach
    nude bathers might consider,
        with a view

of the steelworks three miles off over estuary
    water that is still brown even
        when it is blue...

and a concrete slipway. That's where it crawled,
    creaked and cranked to the sea,
        the *machine* –

quite what, no one will swear to. But there was an
    establishment, with *boffins*, like a wartime
        job creation scheme

for the too-intelligent, not safe to release
    into battle, egghead duffers,
        vaguely innocent

as country parsons... while on its legs,
    tracks or treads or whatever
        it had, down it went

leaving a hippo-fart of bubbles, forging out
    into the mud-mist, in the tide wind,
        over silt fields.

It might be squatting there still – gone native
    with crustaceans? waiting on the hour
        of Britain's need?

glum-struck and sulking, rusting to an outline
    filled with more and more space
        and time to brood

on where their sweet logics would lead us,
    those *boffins*, and how it got out
        while the going was good.

Amphora

sunk unbroken
tipsy-bedded
in the harbour
silt. How long
precisely till the wine

disperses by dilution or in tides'
rinse-dilute-shake-rinse cycle
– homeopathically – grows

like memory, by absence,
to the hundredth power
till each last molecule

in the ocean *knows*
itself as Homer's
wine-dark sea?

Pour

Call it connecting
one moment with another:
                              water-

in-the-glass with water-in-the-jug,
two bodies of water
                         and between,

this slick and fluted glitter,
                                 slightly
arcing, rebraiding itself as it falls,

as for tangible
                  seconds it's a thin
taut string of surface tension

that my hand feels, on the handle,
as a pulse, a pull,
                       a thing

in space, that lives in this world
like us, with purpose
                          though not one

least particle is constant, knows
its place, could account
                            or be held

to account for what it is or does.

The Presence

(Barbara Hepworth, Single Form)

A one. A standing
        on its own plinth. Slim
                slicked naked singularity.
What's with it? All
        the presence it contains,
                silt swirling to the surface,
stops there, while light
        taps, taps from the outside
                and is not admitted. That
assurance, that's what makes me
        want to rattle it – me
                like a Visigoth, all gawp
and grievance, at the sack
        of Rome, left staring
                at boneyards of stone and
(that's what winds us up
        into a rage of looting) and
                where did it go? The presence.
Stepped calmly aside
        like one of the gods they
                only half believe in, smug
as a joke they don't want us
        to get. Well, we
                don't   get   it
and won't, till one sunset smoky
        from the burning towns behind us
                I tether my horse to a stone
and lie back with the sky.
        And the boulder leans in
                at the edge of my sleep
and quite suddenly Oh I
        get it. Always had it, but
                to find it, had to come this weary way.

Globe

(for Gillian Clarke)

on the half-landing newel post, a near-
sphere, scratched and grainy, oiled
with the sweat of our palms,
        our turns and hesitations on the stair,

till it reflects, no, *recollects* us – floor,
doors, ceiling rose and treads and risers
gathered to itself, one seamlessly
        infolded room in which one window,

stretch-flexed like a blown sheet, holds
two poplars and a lamppost, their verticals
drawn like a bow, such fling and snap in them,
        and the wind bounding round the garden

boundless, leaf-snuffling, chasing its tail,
and any glimpse of distances beyond
returns *from the round earth's*
        imagin'd corners, from Einstein's infinity

bearing nearness like travellers' tales
of a land with no borders, where no
nation's name can be pinned,
        a land like a single particular

drop in free fall, us and our
world in it, intricate and in-
conceivable, imperfect,
        whole.

Betweenland V

The most open of borders
   and the most real:
      watershed, an imponderable
  doodle that respects
      no parallel;
no imperial line ruled in the sand
  of deserts. Our bodies feel

the way it's tending,
  as each drop of rain
      discovers – an idea as grand
  as you might expect
      of a mountain,
too exact and simple, almost,
  for the mind to entertain.

We've climbed all day towards it
  in the mist. Light goes.
      Only now, you hear the un-
seen water, tending
      to a new decision. Though
we don't know what it is
  that knows, it knows.

Concentrations

Sit

 quiet
and in time

the mind uncurls
like paper flowers in water.

It is only the idea
of flowers
 which however

(off out of sight
yet never closer)

do exist, as

light does, as does water.

Shift

 slightly
and a floorboard gives,

a syllable, or less:
the timbre of a voice

which states, notwithstanding,
that the floor has knowledge of you,

the flowering-out of load
from where you touch,

just as the air accommodates

(accommodates its slight self to)
your breathing. Yes,

you would be missed.

Drip

    of this moment, and this,

no clock tick, no *points de suspension*,
not a sign-your-name-here dotted line

but each apart
        as a drop in a dark
cave lake, its ripples spreading and

reflect/deflected from the unseen
edges, interference

patterns where they mesh from this
side, this and this, which make

a texture that for want
of words we might call *Me*.

Salt

    taste, unexplaining of itself,
a surprise to the mind from the body,

from the corner of the eye down my cheek
to the tip of my tongue, just a drip

of the litres per day that rain down through us
not to mention
        the mist of you and me
inside the windscreen, or the shadow

on the undersheet: our dispersal
with time into space. We might be drying

out slowly, to a hot and frosty glitter
like a shallow rock pool in the sun.

Heart

       to heartbeat,
these dumb

beasts of burden (each
breath out returning, or a deep

consideration of the small intestine
now and then,
the eyelid's faithful blink)

that carry us
home,
       one foot
behind another, even when

we're sleeping, self-
forgotten,

steady as we go.

Bridge Passages

1 *In Mist*

Slim slung
the struts and wires of it,

the way it sidles
into white midstream

taking just a basic kit
of light and line,

not promising a landfall...
Heavy goods pour on

over into the blank
others seem to return from

so of course we trust it
like an elegant equation.

2 *Murk*

Brown sky over the channel, not
pollution but reflection. Correspondences:
   as below, so above. Today,

with light as if from somewhere
else, the bridge's peppermint-cream
hint-of-neon filaments

rise like a bright idea, against
that collusion – a bridge underwater,
   or the ideal of one, sunk

in the density of things, in material gloom.

3 *Scour*

: the principle that age
and every grain of sand
in flowing water knows,
that every child
       who's stood up to the ankles
       in a back-dragging wave
learns in a yelp

       as the beach becomes live,
       an ants' nest, swarming away
beneath his footsoles: scour,
       as ceaseless as a digging
       animal, scrabbling
back upstream: scour,

       that would bring a grand
       construction project to its knees
       unstrung like a broken guitar
unless we trust our mass
       to long pins, tiny self-
       effacing footings, merest points
of least resistance, going tiptoe.

Betweenland VI

The gulls going home from the city,
from a day's work at the landfill,
this moment everywhere, at once:

the sky is strung with strands of them,
converging out to sea, beyond us –
their vanishing point, the bare

fact of a rock where even the Vikings
left just the hull of a word: *Holm.*
Make of that sound what you will.

The Moveable Island

...shifts, like the hull of a boat
left drifting, grounded on a different shoal
   each morning, in the midway, out
   where the Severn is letting, has let,
itself go into sea, like a thought into sleep:
   now you're there, now you're not.
   Today the outlook's vague, the weather
iffy. *Precipitation within sight: good... Low,*
   losing identity... If God could *dither*
   here's how it would look: these grand
tides like a lesson in bad governance, all power, no
   fixed purpose. No wonder the island
   keeps its distances. Its reticence. Whichever
shore you look from, it seems closer to the other.

   It's an abiding absence: in some
lights, a prison hulk; or, grey mornings after
   the storm, a lighthouse stump;
   a tanker, *stricken* (as they say, as if
the load that leaked, to blight our foreshores,
   was heart's-blood or grief).
   Sometimes it wallows, half
submerged, King Log hauled to and fro in state
   twice a day − a life or afterlife
   beyond us, though you can almost
see a way at lowest tides from shoal to shoal
   stitched with bird-tracks where a soul
not weighted by its body might − but for one last
narrow channel between − might just pass.

   And now I'm closer, in the narrow
focus of my father's old field-glasses, adrift
   on a plain of brown wave-furrows
   till there: a skirt of mud-rock, un-
approachable by any craft, steepens to paler grey,
   with lichen blotches, then green
   above the tide-line, grass, almost

wind-dried, salt-pickled, enough for a castaway
   goat. A self-sufficiency. Or so
   his binoculars say, though what
do they know – army surplus before I was born,
   discharged from the ranks maybe
for just such imaginings: seeing a place that is not
for owning, most there only when you look away?

Betweenland VII

Then again: not a mouth but an ear,

the estuary's battered pewter hearing-trumpet
amplifying distance – closer, suddenly,

a *frisson* of unaccustomed languages,
belowdecks, in hostels, in leave-to-remain

tribunals. Other commodities.
Much that is lost in translation.

And again, here: this so-near-

the-road-and-yet-so-far-from-anywhere
mud-creek with no track to it, windings

as private and intricate as the inner ear,
that feels the whole sea's balance

shift, has no name on the map and
is, possibly, somewhere

not a living soul has been.

Hereinunder

...find the sound of water
not heard – but you'd sit up
   suddenly, not knowing what
had jogged you, if it stopped.

   It's a long-held (from the twig-
clogged, rust-toothed intake grille)
   breath (held beneath flagged
yard and feet and floorboards) till

   in this culvert it blinks back,
with a dark tinge like a cave-
   stream. With an inward look.
How long it's been away

   is just one of its secrets,
like the trickle-down of bedroom
   whispers, creaks and sleep-talk,
those heightened away-from-home

   dreams a strange bed gives you: all
in a night's work to water, like bubble-
   bath, slops and bleach and boiler oil
and what's sluiced from marble

   slab or sponged from carpet:
almost legible, these depositions
   in colourless copperplate
on its surface, shifting, hitching

   like alibis coming undone, spilled
on down to the settling pond
   where they lie in the silt, silt-
coloured, like tench: a weekend
   unaccounted for, time killed.

Betweenland VIII

What my father can't hear, I hear for him – the flow,
the under-hush of water, tide-drag, friction with itself –
though it's only one thread of the chord (too broad, too low

for human ears) the whole estuary is. Or maybe that,
not the chatter of things, *is* what he's left with now
most articulate sound has withdrawn from him, into what

it floats on: de-creation, the Ten Thousand Things
in rips and eddies on its surface, not emptiness but
a labyrinthine plainness of intent – the way water thinks

its one brilliant thought: *falling*. Like him, I clutch
at a word: *falling*, opening a hatch to the clanking
and thud, below decks, of an engine room – such

all-sound that it's silence, or as good as. Vertigo.

Bread and Salt

(for Jonathan and Petra)

Out of the bloodstream steps an old
Estonian. He has waded so far
to bring you this – bread, salt, a threshold
gift, like frankincense and myrrh:
bread the colour of peat
                              (in Lahemaa
I met a bog pool's gaze, its pickled
moss-threads like an iris round its clear
black, its bottomless knowing)
                              and salt
like snow-grit at the roadside, rock-
salt from forced-labour caves where miners
might shrivel and parch and, left for dead,
preserved like salt cod, never rot.
Out of the bloodstream they come to find us
home
          – plain blessings, salt and bread.

Yalta, 1945

Jigging the text, the torn tracts, till they slot
and settle, the inscribers of the coming age
lean back from the table. One folds a page
down, crisply. There'll be i's to dot
etcetera after lunch. Black pips of shot
in purple pigeon breasts (bred in the cage
for shotgun wars the house-guests wage)
are spat discreetly out, bones picked, and what
shudders of moon cross the lawn, what steel
zinging of bats as they stuka the lake...?
The spoils of peace: the drafts and maps discarded,
numbers estimated who will wake to feel
the margins closing, run, sleep rough, take
their chance, ford rivers; the bridges are guarded.

The Grounds

Untenable grounds:

betweenlands dis-
appearing when the tide's attention

is elsewhere, recurrent dreams

devoid of incident or
anyone. (That fact alone

seems to be saying something.)

        Indefinite grounds:

        constant inconstancy.
        Birds appear, condensing

        from the sky where they had been

        and not been, incipient, un-
        formed, latent, like silt,

        say, in this ever-flexing water.

Indefinable grounds:

don't try to set foot,
not even if some craft

could steady in these mud-thick shallows

(almost ground) by ground
almost as loose as water. Don't

count on your fine distinctions then.

Irrefutable grounds

we can't possess, but maps
and I can name them... Here:

Welsh Ground, The English Stones,

*The Scars, Goblin Ledge, The Near
Deep, Gruggy...* (One of those

is mine to keep. I made it.)

Six hours, and the grounds

are remembered. Forgotten. Remembered
as matt against dazzle or when the sea

roughs up, slick-sheened – as regular

as breathing (no two breaths the same),
as sure a foundation for our coming-

goings as the flesh we age in,

        as the (mortgaged) ground beneath our feet.

To Build a Bridge

One way would be matter, braced to bear
the thud and hiss of traffic, day by day;
the other, a mere force field traced in air,

the essence of a bridge, almost not there
on days when mist directs *Dissolve to grey*.
One way, we'd be matter, braced to bear

(though what's born leaves us standing: wear,
tear, tariff, we're our children's carriageway),
the other, a mere force field traced in air

which would be nothing if we didn't share
a footing in the silt, the under-clay.
One way we're matter, braced to bear

the space around us, distance leading where
we won't go, planted in the mud to stay.
The other, a mere force field traced in air

draws its conclusions, whispering: Just dare
to trust your weight to nothing and...away!
Or: *One* Way. Still we matter, braced to bear
each other: you, me, force fields traced in air.

Betweenland IX

There's a river underneath the river:
the lowest of tides make that clear –

with broad meanders, floodplain
pastures like our own upstream

but monochrome, an early silver-
nitrate plate that flicks to negative

and back, depending how you tilt it,

a memento of itself, or what
we had forgotten we'd forgotten,

the original land we knew before
the first foot- or hoof-print, before

the astonishment of grass, before
there was a way to know *before*.

First Things

Never more than a blink away
from first things… It seems only today

that Washing Machine Dreaming
opened its timeless tracts to me,
its spiral galaxy

expanding at nine hundred revs per minute
like a brisk shake from the One Dog
back from splashing in eternity.

It's a whorl in the long grass
where a little twister did its pirouette

or the same Dog, in its next-door's
yappy spaniel form,
turned three times widdershins

with its every ancestor on great savannahs
where it goes to dream
and we are no more

than a smudge of smoke
on the horizon.

Elderly Iceberg off the Esplanade

Last night it came knocking, a first
since the end of the Ice Age. A stray eddy brought it,
a backhander from the Gulf Stream. It was heading
                              inland, could it be to spawn?

It had jumped ship from the loosening Arctic.
Was a waster, pock-marked, sunken-featured,
in its mud mac. Lurked in the sea lane, only wanted love.
                              Was a monster, unnaturally born

from the wreck of a thousand-tonne reefer.
Unassuming little thing, it was huge
in no definite sense. Past help, on the edge of extinction,
                              it still had it in it to bite

beneath the waterline. It was a blatant falsehood;
admitted as much to your face. Call it a bad dream
if you like but when I looked this morning
                              it was still in sight

trapped in a tide pool, half a mile out
on the silt you can't trust your weight to,
not to bear you, not to let you go.
                              It was all I could do

not to wade out and follow. It wasn't the last,
just a message from last-ness, a crumpled
brown parcel from an unsuspected
                              awful aunt who might

just turn up any day to stay. Naturally
it was impossible; such things have to be
believed – *quia impossibile est.*
                              That species of *true.*

Don't breathe a word of this;
they'll be heaving it out, to *preserve.* Let it go.
This world should not detain it.
                              It would do the same for you.

Meander

               which is anything
          but indirection.
The river desires

with a fixed and single-
               minded purpose
          to be everywhere,

every drop of it free

to fall into conversation
               with a loose
          grain here, a slow-

eroding seepage there,
of possibility –

               such gentle rigour
          with raggy pink balsam
at its edges, gasholders beyond

and the plosh of a rat shape

               into water
          eddying away
also part of the argument:

we shall return to this,
               later,

          no hurry,
but we shall return.

Thinks Bubble

Too-early-to-be-early time, too late
to be late: that time you wake in
with no edges:
                a thin perturbation
of birds way out in the dark
on mud banks in mid channel,

something in the offing, not
(like, say, an *understanding*)
yet, or ever, *come to*

as if there was *somewhere else*
a thought might be

*

(which, by some life-
preserving instinct, has to hide
from its own prying eyes)

*

Thought: a noun
in the past tense.

Now, how to conceive
/ to conceive of

the future…? (Leave
the present to one side, for now.)

*

In the forty-years-ago
chess congress
where the danger was
I might have won,

a hundred old men
and unnaturally still
stern boys bent
cranium to cranium,

their two-faced clocks
between them, three hours in
and silence gathering
as for an execution.

                     Whack
of the door: *Oy! Wake up!*
                        And plump
laughing Buddha ran off down the corridor.

(By the time they caught him he was just a kid again.)

*

Or imagine the stone

young not-yet-Doctor Johnson might have socked
over the wall into the Berkeleys' garden. *Please*

can I have my stone back? How, boy, says the not-
yet-Bishop's father, when there is no

such object? Be off, and while you're at it
take this sound of breaking glass.

*

Thinks was easy to conceive:
a bubble

in the Beano, scalloped edges
like a cloud –

a meaning gathering. It might
precipitate.

Soon I learned how it fell
into text – slant, side-blown,
as italics.

      Rain now
falls on water, in the small hours,

as a tree in the forest, as *thinks*
not quite *thought*

returns itself seamlessly
into itself,

the mind, the weary mind,
not there to see.

*

The mud bank, loosening
from inside: the tide begins to fill
the prints the birds have left

with light.

For this moment, this moment alone
it's a mud-reader's dream,

dissolving. The Rosetta Stone.

*

The A to Z, gone threadbare
at the folds...
          Don't let go
of my hand –
          we could slip through.

*

Oh, trusty mind, old friend, won't take no
for an answer, insisting on walking us home,

its pencil-torch beam all we see
as dark recoils to darker round it,

faithful mind, can't stop telling us
how we mustn't worry;

it's going to talk to us, *all* the way there.

*

And the birds
are not here. Are not
the ones I saw or thought
I saw last evening. Not any that might

soon appear,
specks of less-than-
darkness against dark, or dark
against the estuary's new flat light.

Are not
    sight, sound
        or birds. Are
            nothing, and yet

            that takes flight.

Betweenland X

Just after sunset, and the tide
high, almost white, dull–
lambent like nothing the sky

holds or could lend it. Each
shore, this and that shore,
black, a particular

blackness pinned in place
by each house- or street-lamp.
Done with. As if land

was night, and us its night-thoughts
and the river was the draining down
of daylight, westwards and out

of the world, so how could you not
(your gaze at least) feel drawn
and want, half want, to follow?

Ice Man Dreaming

1

Somewhere right now he might be groaning,
    waking. It's been no time where he's been,
in the grand slow downhill slalom. Jolt.

Where was I? A dim panic: what passed
for life, the scrabbling before the calm,
    coming back like an ache. A loosening

in the cells. Blood, sluggishly seething
    like the spring melt. It's too soon,
he can't uncurl yet. Old leathery foetus,

    he's hundreds of years before term,
half-sucked sweet on the glacier's tongue,
    eye mucus thinning for the first blink. *No,*

not this dream, please, I want the other one…

2

where we lift off, sloughing the blur of the runway,
    our slowed-down and overcast lives. Streaming mist,
        then we're clear, we've punched clean into heaven: snow-

dazzle plains of stratocumulus around us, the palaeo-arctic
    of the edge of space, and if there are angels they'll be hide-
        clad hunters, stooped, numb, following tracks in the light.

It's as clear as *déjà vu*: the ice-sheet's great simplicities,
    the page before words, where each sharpened sight and smell
        and spear tip made its point. We trudged into the dream-

time, deeper, and even the wolf frieze on the skyline watched,
    uneasy, to see what we'd become. *Fasten your seatbelts, please,*
        the pilot's crackle wakes me. *We may be in for a little*

turbulence. We hit, really *hit*, a pocket of substantial air…

3

       as if we'd tripped on an isobar. Aren't there jolts
      and judders every day, like the digital twitch
   that slips off wavelength, freezes (pixel blocks
like shattered windscreen) then resumes? A child,

       I thought the world was a beach ball in its safe
      string-bag of latitude and longitude. The lines stretch
   and pull out of shape. Stay home or take flight, jet lag
will come to find you, seasons fraying at the edges,

       threads of bird-flocks coming loose; the implausible
      white stab that's an ibis on a mud flat; or the swifts
   high up, at the limits of hearing crying *flee, flee!*
early, few. It's too soon to say this represents a trend.

       By the time we can, don't worry, it will be too late...

4

       to tell the future. Read my palm.
      Or the prints, like tiny anticyclones
   googlied in off the Atlantic,

       we leave wherever we've touched,
      with the glisten of sweat
   a polygraph would twitch at. Is

       it hot in here or is it me?
      With a gargling crunch
   my American fridge-freezer

       calves me a tumblerful
      of crushed ice for the poolside weather
   we would fly a thousand miles for,

       wouldn't we: a dream...

5

as far off and puzzling, abruptly, as the one
in which I was the ice man, or a man
    the ice had dreamed before its creeping fever

woke it in a sweat. Come to earth with a bump
    on newly-bare grit pastures, he's tipped out,
tipsy, swaying upright, stumbling downhill

    where the water in him leads – *Where was I,*
where had I been going? – the burn of the air
    in his raw voice box crackling no language

anybody understands, through the turned
    backs of outskirts, without papers or leave
to remain (the ice in him still weeping) and

    into the heart of the town, somewhere, now.

Petroglyphs

(Old Zalavruga, Belomorsk district, Karelia)

Five thousand years from now
    will we have left one sign
        as plain and brave as these

three, pecked by hand (think how
    long) from the granite, line
        abreast on palaeolithic skis

coming from silence, from the wake
    of an Ice Age, towards us (yes,
        us) through blots and blurs of snow,

through not forgetting, through the work
    of hands, through three-togetherness,
        through the motionless blizzard of stone?

Dead Letter Box

This moment – full stop, and a breath
to let the ink dry... or this –

folding the paper too precisely, as if
a life depended on it... or this –

your lick on the gummed flap
sealed, your DNA preserved in it –

are small rehearsals for the final
letting go – your fingertips

trusting the package to the cool
damp of the hollow tree,

the mercy of woodlice and in time
a stranger's touch, one who will seem

to happen to be passing, walking
the dog whose name is Alibi.

Severn Song
(for John Karl Gross)

The Severn was brown and the Severn was blue –
not this-then-that, not either-or,
no mixture. Two things can be true.
The hills were clouds and the mist was a shore.

The Severn was water, the water was mud
whose eddies stood and did not fill,
the kind of water that's thicker than blood.
The river was flowing, the flowing was still,

the tide-rip the sound of dry fluttering wings
with waves that did not break or fall.
We were two of the world's small particular things.
We were old, we were young, we were no age at all,

for a moment not doing, nor coming undone –
words gained, words lost, till who's to say
which was the father, which was the son,
a week, or fifty years, away.

But the water said *earth* and the water said *sky*.
We were everyone we'd ever been or would be,
every angle of light that says *You*, that says *I*,
and the sea was the river, the river the sea.